SP   I

Phra   .ids

AA

About this book

Jane Wightwick
had the idea

Wina Gunn
wrote the pages

Leila & Zeinah Gaafar
(aged 10 and 12) drew the
first pictures in
each chapter

Robert Bowers
(aged 52) drew the other
pictures, and designed
the book

Ana Bremon

did the Spanish stuff

Important things that
must be included

© g-and-w publishing 2019

A CIP catalogue record for this book is available from
the British Library

ISBN 978-0-7495-8171-8

Published by AA Media Limited, whose registered office
is Grove House, Lutyens Close, Basingstoke, Hampshire
RG24 8AG. Registered number 06112600.

Printed in UK by MRC Print Ltd.

A05742

What's inside

Making friends

How to be cool with the group

Wanna play?

Our guide to joining in everything from hide-and-seek to the latest electronic game

Feeling hungry

Order your favourite foods or go local

Looking good

Make sure you keep up with all those essential fashions

Hanging out

At the pool, beach, or theme park – don't miss out on the action

Pocket money

Spend it here!

Grown-up talk

blah!
blah!
blah!
blah!

If you really, really have to!

Extra stuff

All the handy things – numbers, months, time, days of the week

my big brother
mi hermano mayor

👄 mee airmano my-yor

dad
papá

👄 pa-pah

grandpa
abuelo

👄 abwelo

grandma
abuela

👄 abwela

mum mamá

👄 ma-mah

my little sister
mi hermana pequeña

👄 mee airmana

pekenya

MAKING FRIENDS

Half a step this way

stepfather/stepmother
padrastro/madrastra
👄 padrastro/madrastra

stepbrother/stepsister
hermanastro/hermanastra
👄 airmanastro/airmanastra

half brother/half sister
medio hermano/medio hermana
👄 medyo airmano/
medyo airmana

Hi!
¡Hola!
👄 ola

What's your name?
¿Cómo te llamas?
👄 komo tay yamas

My name's ...
Me llamo ...
👄 may yamo

The Spanish put an upside-down question mark before a question, as well as one the right way up at the end. It's the same with exclamation marks.

¿Isn't that weird? ¡You bet!

Are you OK?
¿Estás bien?
estas beeyen

Cool, and you?
Guay, ¿y tú?
gwhy. ee too

Where are you from?
¿De dónde eres?
day donday air-res

from Canada

de Canadá

🫦 day canadah

from Ireland

de Irlanda

🫦 day eerlanda

from Scotland

de Escocia

🫦 day escothya

from Wales del País de Gales

🫦 del pie-yis day gal-les

That means "the land of the Gauls".

from the United States

de los Estados Unidos

🫦 day los estados ooneedos

from England

de Inglaterra

🫦 day eengla-tairra

10

Los SMS

H! K acs?
qnd qdms
xa jgar fnd?
m1ml xfa A2

Bet you're thinking — those Spanish texts don't make sense! But remember: a Spanish 2 is pronounced 'dos', the letter 'K' is 'kay' and 'A' is 'ah'. The Spanish word for 'times' as in 2x2 is 'por', so 'por favor' (please) becomes 'xfa'. Get it now? … K RSA!

H! (¡hola!)
hiya!

K acs? (¿que haces?)
UOK?

K RSA (que risa)
LOL

fnd (fin de semana)
w/end

xfa (por favor)
plz

qnd qdms (cuando quedamos)
wen r we meetn

A2 (adiós)
CU

jgar (jugar)
play

m1ml (mandame un mensaje luego)
txt me

xa (para)
4

11

Star signs

AQUARIUS

Jan. 21 – Feb. 19
Acuario 🗣 akwaree-o

PISCES
Feb. 20 – Mar. 20
Piscis 🗣 pees-thees

ARIES
Mar. 21 – Apr. 20
Aries 🗣 a-rees

TAURUS
Apr. 21 – May. 21
Tauro 🗣 towro

GEMINI

May 22 – June 21
Géminis 🗣 hemeenees

CANCER
June 22 – July 23
Cáncer 🗣 kanthair

LEO
July 24 – Aug. 23
Leo 🗣 leo

VIRGO
Aug. 24 – Sep. 23
Virgo 🗣 beergo

LIBRA
Sep. 24 – Oct. 23
Libra 🗣 leebra

SCORPIO
Oct. 24 – Nov. 22
Escorpio 🗣 eskorpee-o

SAGITTARIUS
Nov. 23 – Dec. 21
Sagitario 🗣 sa-heetaree-o

CAPRICORN

Dec. 22 – Jan. 20
Capricornio 🗣 kapreecornee-o

13

football el fútbol
👄 el footbol

rollerblading
el patinaje en línea
👄 el patee-nahay
en leenya

music
la música
👄 la mooseeka

electronic games
los juegos electrónicos
👄 los hway-gos elektroneekos

tv
la tele
👄 la taylay

comics
los tebeos
👄 los taybayos

spiders las arañas
👄 las aranyas

school
el colegio
👄 el kolay-heeyo

15

What's your ...?

¿Cuál es tu ...?

👄 kwal es too ...

favourite group

grupo preferido

👄 groopo prefereedo

favourite colour

color preferido

👄 kol-lor prefereedo

Page 69 →

favourite game

juego preferido

👄 hway-go prefereedo

favourite food

comida preferida

👄 komeeda prefereeda

favourite ringtone

tono preferido

👄 tone-oh prefereedo

favourite animal

animal preferido

👄 anee-mal prefereedo

favourite team

equipo preferido

👄 ekeepo prefereedo

Talk about your pets

He's hungry

Está hambriento

🗣 esta ambree-yento

Can I stroke your dog?

¿Puedo acariciar tu perro?

🗣 pwedo atharee-thyar

too pair-ro

She's sleeping

Está durmiendo

🗣 esta doormee-yendo

Do you have any pets?

¿Tienes alguna mascota?

🗣 tee-enes algoona

mascota

dog
el perro
🗣 el pair-ro

cat
el gato
🗣 el gato

snake
la serpiente
🗣 la serpee-entay

guinea pig
la cobaya
🗣 la kob-eye-a

hamster
el hámster
🗣 el hamstair

parakeet
el periquito
🗣 el peree-keeto

My little doggy goes *guau guau!*

A Spanish doggy (that's "guauguau" in baby language) doesn't say "woof, woof", it says *"guau, guau"* (*gwa-oo, gwa-oo*). A Spanish bird says *"pío, pío"* (*pee-o, pee-o*) and "cock-a-doodle-do" in Spanish chicken-speak is *"kikirikí"* (*kee-kee ree-kee*). But a cat does say *"miaow"* and a cow *"moo"* whether they're speaking Spanish or English!

19

Talk about school (if you can stand it)

geography
la geografía
👄 la heogra-feeya

PE
la gimnasia
👄 la heem-naseeya

art
el dibujo artístico
👄 el deebooho arteesteeko

Spanish
m.smith
form 2b

Spanish
el español
👄 el espanyol

maths
las mates
👄 las mat-tes

music
la música
🗣 la mooseeka

English
el inglés
🗣 el eeng-les

history
la historia
🗣 la eestoreeya

science
las naturales
🗣 las natoorar-les

21

IT

TI

 tay-ee

Way unfair!

Spanish children hardly ever have to wear uniform to school and have very long holidays: 10 weeks in the summer and another 5–6 weeks throughout the rest of the year. But before you turn green with envy, you might not like the mounds of *"deberes para las vacaciones"* (*debair-res para las bakathee-yones*), that's "vacation homework"! And if you fail your exams, the teachers could make you repeat the whole year with your little sister!

Talk about your phone

That's ancient
¡Qué anticuado!
🗣 kay antee-kwado

I've run out of credit
Me he quedado sin saldo
🗣 may ay kay-dado seen saldo

What's your mobile phone like?
¿Cómo es tu móvil?
🗣 komo es too mo-beel

Lucky!
¡Qué suerte!
🗣 kay swair-tay

What a cool ringtone!
¡Qué tono más chulo!
🗣 kay tone-oh mass choolo

23

Gossip

Can you keep a secret?

¿Puedes guardar un secreto?

👄 pwedes gwardar oon sekreto

Do you have a boyfriend (a girlfriend)?

¿Tienes novio (novia)?

👄 tee-enes nobyo (nobya)

An OK guy/An OK girl

Un tío majo/Una tía maja

👄 oon teeyo maho/ oona teeya maha

What a bossy-boots!

¡Qué mandón!

👄 kay man-don

He/She's nutty!

¡Está como una cabra!

👄 esta komo oona kabra

That means "He/She's like a goat"!

I'm not like that at all!

What a misery guts!

¡Qué malasombra!

👄 kay malas-sombra

You won't make many friends saying this!

Shut up!
¡Cállate!
🗨 kigh-yatay

Bog off!
¡Vete a la porra!
🗨 betay a la porra

If you're fed up with someone, and you want to say something like "you silly …!" or "you stupid …!", you can start with **"pedazo de"** (which actually means "piece of …") and add anything you like. What about …

Stupid banana!
¡Pedazo de plátano!
(pedatho day platano)

or …

Silly sausage!
¡Pedazo de salchicha! (pedatho day salcheecha)

Take your pick. It should do the trick. You could also try **"¡pedazo de idiota!"** (pedatho day eedee-ota). You don't need a translation here, do you?

25

You might have to say

Bother!

¡Ostras!

🗣 os-stras

That means "Oysters"!

Rats!

¡Porras!

🗣 porras

"Did someone call us?"

That's not funny

No tiene gracia

🗣 no tee-enay gra-theeya

That's plenty!

¡Ya vale!

🗣 ya balay

I'm fed up

¡Estoy harto! (boys)

¡Estoy harta! (girls)

🗣 estoy arto/estoy arta

Stop!

¡No hagas eso!

🗣 no agas eso

I want to go home!

¡Me quiero ir a casa!

🗣 may kyairo eer ah kassa

I don't care

Me da igual

🗣 may da eegwal

At last!

¡Por fin!

🗣 por feen

27

Saying goodbye

Here's my address
Aquí tienes mi dirección
👄 akee tee-enes mee

deerek-thyon

What's your address?
¿Cuál es tu dirección?
👄 kwal es too deerek-thyon

Come to visit me
Ven a visitarme
👄 ben a beesee-tarmay

Have a good trip!

¡Buen viaje!

👄 bwen bee-ahay

Write to me soon

Escríbeme pronto

👄 eskree-bemay pronto

Send me a text

Envíame un SMS

👄 envee-armay oon "SMS"

Let's chat online

¿Chateamos?

👄 chatay-amos

Bye!

¡Adiós

👄 adeeyos

What's your email address?

¿Cuál es tu mail?

👄 kwal es too mail

⅂▢@3◇*@ℓ.com

WANNA PLAY?

el elástico
🗨 el elasteeko

el ping-pong
🗨 el "ping-pong"

MP3 player
el reproductor
👄 el raypro-
dooktor

el yo-yó
👄 el "yo yo"

el móvil
👄 el mo-beel

WANNA PLAY?

Do you want to play ...?
¿Quieres jugar ...?
🗨 keyair-res hoogar

... table football?
... al futbolín?
🗨 al footboleen

... cards?
... a las cartas?
🗨 a las kartas

... on the computer?
... con el ordenador?
🗨 kon el orden-ador

... noughts and crosses?
... a las tres en raya?
🗨 a las trays en righ-ya

32

Fancy a game of **foal** or **donkey**?!

In Spain, you don't play "leap frog", you play "foal" – *el potro*. There is also a group version of this called "donkey" – *el burro*. This involves two teams. Team 1 line up in a row with their heads down in the shape of a donkey. Team 2 take it in turns to leap as far as they can onto the back of the "donkey". If the donkey falls over, Team 2 win. If Team 2 touch the ground or can't leap far enough to get all the team on, then Team 1 win – got that?! Spanish children will try to tell you this is enormous fun, but your parents might not be so keen on the bruises!

Can my friend play too?

¿Mi amigo también puede jugar?

mee ameego tam–byen
pway–day hoogar

I have to ask my parents

Se lo tengo que pedir a mis padres

say loe tengo kay pedeer
ah mees padrays

Make yourself heard

Who dares?

You're it!

¡La quedas tú!

🗨 la kedas too

Race you!

¿Una carrera?

🗨 oona karraira

I'm first

Soy el primero (boys)

Soy la primera (girls)

🗨 soy el preemairo

soy la preemaira

37

Electronic games

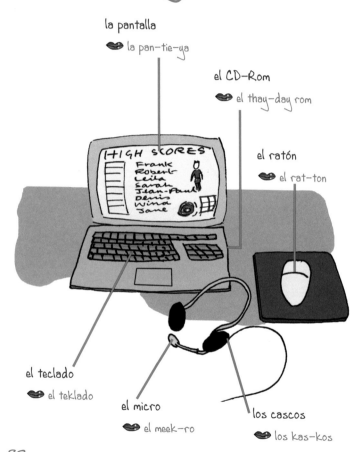

la pantalla
🗨 la pan-tie-ya

el CD-Rom
🗨 el thay-day rom

el ratón
🗨 el rat-ton

el teclado
🗨 el teklado

el micro
🗨 el meek-ro

los cascos
🗨 los kas-kos

Show me

Enséñame

 ensay-nyamay

What do I do?

¿Qué hay que hacer?

kay eye kay athair

Am I dead?

¿Me han matado?

may an matado

Shoot-em-up!

¡Dispárales!

deespar-ralayz

How many lives do I have?

¿Cuántas vidas tengo?

kwantas beedas tengo

How many levels are there?

¿Cuántos niveles hay?

kwantos neebay-les eye

It's virtual fun!

Do you have WiFi?
¿Tienes wifi?

teeyenes weefee
Make sure you say it like this to avoid blank looks!

Send me a message.
Mándame un mensaje.

How do i join?
¿Cómo me apunto?

I'm not old enough.
No tengo edad suficiente.

I'm not allowed.
No tengo permiso.

I don't know who you are.
No te conozco.

my blog
mi blog
🗨 mee blog

my friends
mis amigos
🗨 mees ameegos

my photos
mis fotos
🗨 mees fotos

my videos
mis videos
🗨 mees bee-dayos

my music mi música
🗨 mee mooseeka

Non couch-potato activities!

tennis
el tenis
🗣 el tenees

trampolining
el trampolín
🗣 el "trampoline"

bowling
los bolos
🗣 los bol-los

swimming
la natación
🗣 la nata-thyon

hockey

el hockey

👄 el "hockey"

gymnastics

la gimnasia

👄 la heem-nasya

ballet

el ballet

👄 el ballay

basketball

el baloncesto

👄 el ballon-thesto

and, of course, we haven't forgotten *"el fútbol"*… (P.T.O.)   43

football

boots

las botas

👄 las botas

football kit

el equipo de fútbol

👄 el ekeepo day footbol

ref

el árbitro

👄 el arbeetro

shin pads

las espinilleras

👄 las espinee-yeras

Good save!

¡Vaya parada!

👄 baya parada

Pass! ¡Pasa!

👄 pasa

Offside!
¡Offside!
👄 just say it!

Hands!
¡Mano!
👄 mano

You're on
my team
Tú estás
en mi equipo
👄 too estas en mee ekeepo

crossbar
el larguero
👄 el largairo

goalpost
el palo
👄 el pallo

goal
el gol
👄 el gol

goalie
el portero
👄 el portairo

45

46

Keeping the others in line

Not like that!

¡Así no!

👄 asee no

You cheat! ¡Tramposo! (boys only)

¡Tramposa! (girls only)

👄 tramposo/tramposa

I'm not playing anymore

Ya no juego

👄 ya no hwego

It's not fair!

¡No es justo!

👄 no es hoosto

Stop it!

¡No hagas eso!

👄 no agas eso

47

Showing off

... do a handstand?
... hacer el pino?
🗨 athair el peeno

Can you ...
¿Sabes ...
🗨 sabays

Look at me!
¡Mírame!
🗨 meera-may

... do a cartwheel?
... dar volteretas laterales?
🗨 dar boltair-retas latairal-les

... do this?
... hacer esto?
🗨 athair esto

Impress your Spanish friends with this!

You can show off to your new Spanish friends by practising this tongue twister:

Tres tristes tigres comían trigo en un trigal.

trays treestays teegrays comee-an treego en oon treegal

(This means "Three sad tigers ate wheat in a wheat field".)

Then see if they can do as well with this English one:

"She sells seashells on the seashore, but the shells she sells aren't seashells, I'm sure."

For a rainy day

pack of cards
una baraja de cartas
👄 oona baraha day kartas

my deal/your deal
yo doy/tú das
👄 yo doy/too das

king
el rey
👄 el ray

queen
la reina
👄 la ray-eena

jack
la jota
👄 la hota

joker
el komodín
👄 el komodeen

tréboles
👄 trebol-les

corazones
👄 korazon-nes

picas
👄 peekas

diamantes
👄 dee-amantays

50

Do you have the ace of swords?!

You might also see Spanish children playing with a different pack of cards. There are only 48 cards instead of 52 and the suits are also different. Instead of clubs, spades, diamonds and hearts, there are gold coins (*oros*), swords (*espadas*), cups (*copas*) and batons (*bastos*).

chessboard el tablero
👄 el tablairo

bishop el alfil
👄 el alfeel

pawn el peón
👄 el pay-on

king el rey
👄 el ray

queen la reina
👄 la ray-eena

rook
la torre
👄 la torray

knight el caballo
👄 el kab-eye-o

51

FEELING HUNGRY

hamburger
la hamburguesa
🗣 la amboorgaysa

chips
las patatas fritas
🗣 las patatas freetas

ice cream
el helado
🗣 el elardo

coke
una coca
🗣 oona koka

squid
los calamares
🗨 los kalamar-res

creme caramel
el flan
🗨 el flan
(Watch out! "Flan" in Spanish doesn't mean a pastry tart with cheese!)

la paella
🗨 la pie-eyya

orange juice
el zumo de naranja
🗨 el thoomo day
naran-ha

Grub

I'm starving

Tengo un hambre de lobo

👄 tengo oon ambray day lobo

That means "I have the hunger of a wolf"!

el lobo

Please can I have ...

Por favor, me da ...

👄 por fabor, may da

... a croissant

un cruasán

oon krwasan

... a cream bun

un bollo con nata

oon boyo kon nata

... a puff pastry

una palmera

oona palmayra

... a waffle

un gofre

oon go-fray

... a muffin

una magdalena

oona magda-layna

los churros

 los choorros

These are wonderful sugary doughnut-like snacks. They are sold in cafés and kiosks and usually come in a paper cone. They are also very popular for breakfast in winter, with thick hot chocolate (**chocolate con churros**).

You: Can I have some churros, Mum?

Mum: No. They'll make you fat and rot your teeth.

You: But I think it's good to experience a foreign culture through authentic local food.

Mum: Oh, all right then.

Churros? *"¡Mm, mm!"*, Garlic sandwich? *"¡Agh!"*. If you're going to make foody noises you'll need to know how to do it properly in Spanish! "Yum, yum!" is out in Spanish. You should say *"¡Mm, mm!"*. And "Yuk!" is *"¡Agh!"* (pronounced *"ag"*), but be careful not to let adults hear you say this!

Drink up

I'm dying for
a drink

Me muero de sed

🗣 may mwero
day sed

I'd like ...

Me apetece ...

🗣 may apay-taythay

... a coke

... una coca

🗣 oona koka

... an orange juice

... un zumo de naranja

🗣 oon thoomo day naran-ha

... an apple juice

... un zumo de manzana

🗣 oon thoomo day
manthana

57

... a lemonade

una Fanta® de limón

🗨 oona Fanta
day leemon

In Spain ask for **una Fanta® de limón** when you want a lemonade or **Fanta® de naranja** (*fanta day naran-ha*) for a fizzy orange. Fanta® is the most popular type and so that's what people say.

... water agua

🗨 agwa

... a milkshake

... un batido

🗨 oon bateedo

You get your hot chocolate in a large cup (to dunk your churros in).

... a hot chocolate
... un chocolate
🗨 oon chokolatay

58

59

Tap into *Tapas*

There's a perfect way to try a little bit of everything in Spain and that's *"tapas"*. These are little snacks that everyone eats in cafés and bars (which the adults might insist on going to). *Tapas* come in little dishes and are a great way of finding out if you like something without risking a torrent of abuse if you leave an expensive meal untouched.

Here are four of the most popular:

tortilla

🗣 tortee-ya
Spanish omelette – thick and comes in slices

croquetas
🗣 kroketas
egg-shaped rissoles filled with chicken, ham or fish

albóndigas
🗣 albon-deegas
meatballs in tomato sauce

calamares a la romana
🗣 kalamar-res a la romana
squid rings

Parties

balloon el globo
👄 el glow-bo

Can I have some more?
¿Puedo tener un poco más?
👄 pwaydo tenair oon poko mas

party hat
el gorro de fiesta
👄 el gorro day fee-esta

This is for you
Esto es para ti
👄 esto es para tee

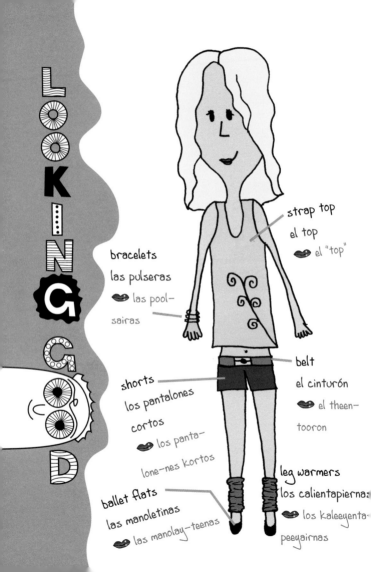

LOOKING GOOD

strap top
el top
💋 el "top"

bracelets
las pulseras
💋 las pool-sairas

belt
el cinturón
💋 el theen-tooron

shorts
los pantalones cortos
💋 los panta-lone-nes kortos

ballet flats
las manoletinas
💋 las manolay-teenas

leg warmers
los calientapiernas
💋 los kaleeyenta-peeyairnas

cap
la gorra
la gorra

earphones
los auriculares
los owree-
koolar-res

hoodie
la capucha
la kapoocha

jeans
los vaqueros
los bakayros

trainers
las deportivas
las daypor-teebas

LOOKING GOOD

Clothes

jeans
los vaqueros
💋 los bakayros

sweatshirt
la sudadera
💋 la sooda-dayra

T-shirt
la camiseta
💋 la kameeseta

football shirt
la camiseta de fútbol
💋 la kameeseta day footbol

trainers
las deportivas
💋 las daypor-teebas

shoes
los zapatos
💋 los thapatos

dress
el traje
🫦 el trahay

skirt
la falda
🫦 la falda

trousers
los pantalones
🫦 los panta-lone-nes

A pair of cowboys?

The word for jeans in Spanish (**los vaqueros** – los bakayros) actually means "cowboys" because they were the first people to wear these trousers.

That T-shirt, please
Esa camiseta, por favor
🫘 esa kameeseta, por fabor

Cool tattoo!
¡Qué calcamonía más chula!
🫘 kay kalka-moneeya mass choola

The pink frilly one
La rosa con volantitos
🫘 la rosa kon bolanteetos

Awesome miniskirt!
¡Vaya minifalda mas chula!
🫘 baya meenee falda mass choola

The purple stripey one
La morada de rayas
🫘 la morada day righ-yas

spotty
de lunares

🗣 day loonar-res

flowery
de flores

🗣 day flor-res

frilly
con volantitos

🗣 kon bolanteetos

glittery
con brillos

🗣 kon breeyos

stripey
de rayas

🗣 day righ-yas

Make it up!

lip gloss
el Brillo de labios

🗨 el breeyo day labyos

glitter gel
la brillantina

🗨 la breeyan–teena

nail varnish
el pintauñas

🗨 el peentaw–nyas

earrings los pendientes

🗨 los pend–yentays

I need a mirror
Necesito un espejo

🗨 netthayseeto oon espay–ho

eye shadow
la sombra de ojos

🗨 la sombray day o–hos

Can I borrow your straighteners?
¿Me dejas tu alisador de pelo?

🗨 may day–has too alee–sadoor day pay–lo

colours

los colores

💋 los kolor-res

Colour this page yourself (you can't expect us to do everything!)

white
blanco
💋 blanko

blue
azul
💋 athool

green
verde
💋 berday

pink
rosa
💋 rossa

yellow amarillo
💋 amareeyo

orange
naranja
💋 naranha

purple morado
💋 morado

red
rojo
💋 roho

black
negro
💋 naygro

69

What should we do?

¿Qué hacemos?

👄 kay athay-mos

Can I come?

¿Puedo ir?

👄 pwedo eer

Where do you all hang out?

¿Por dónde salís vosotros?

👄 por donday salees bos-otros

That's really wicked

Eso es chachi

👄 eso es chachee

I'm (not) allowed

(No) me dejan

👄 (no) may day-han

72

Let's go back Regresemos

💋 regray-saymos

That gives me goose bumps (or "chicken flesh" in Spanish!)

Eso me pone la carne de gallina

💋 eso may ponay la karnay day gayeena

I'm bored to death

Me muero de aburrimiento

💋 may mwero day aburree-mee-ento

HOUSE OF MIRRORS

That's a laugh

Te ríes cantidad

💋 tay reeyes kanteedad

Beach babes

Can I borrow this?

¿Me dejas esto?

🗣 may dehas esto

Let's hit the beach

Vamos a la playa

🗣 bamos a la playa

Is this your bucket?

¿Es tuyo este cubo?

🗣 es tooyo

🗣 estay koobo

You can bury me

Me puedes enterrar

🗣 pay pwedes entair-rar

Stop throwing sand!

¡Deja de echar arena!

🗣 dayha day echar arayna

Mind my eyes!

¡Cuidado con mis ojos!

🗣 kweedado kon mees ohos

sandcastle
el castillo de arena
🗣 el casteeyo day arayna

sea
el mar
🗣 el mar

beach la playa
🗣 la playa

towel
la toalla
🗣 la toe-aya

swimming costume
el bañador
🗣 el banyador

bucket el cubo
🗣 el koobo

snorkel
el tubo
🗣 el toobo

shells
las conchas
🗣 las konchas

spade
la pala
🗣 la palla

75

It's going swimmingly!

How to make a splash in Spanish!

Let's hit the swimming pool

Vamos a la piscina

🗣 bamos a la peeseena

Can you swim (underwater)?

¿Sabes nadar (debajo del agua)? 🗣 sabays nadar (debaho del agwa)

Me too/I can't

Yo también/Yo no

🗣 yo tambeeyen/ yo no

Can you dive?

¿Te sabes tirar de cabeza?

🗣 tay sabays teerar day kabaytha

I'm getting changed

Me estoy cambiando

🗣 may estoy kambee-ando

Can you swim ...?
¿Sabes nadar ...?
👄 sabays nadar

... backstroke
a espalda
👄 a espalda

... butterfly
a mariposa
👄 a mareeposa

... crawl
a crol
👄 a krol

... breaststroke
a braza 👄 a bratha

slide
el tobogán
👄 el tobogan

goggles
las gafas
👄 las gafas

Downtown

Do you know the way?
¿Te sabes el camino?
💬 tay sabays el kameeno

Pooper-scoopers on wheels!

You might see bright green-and-white motorcycles with funny vacuum cleaners on the side riding around town scooping up the dog poop. The people riding the bikes look like astronauts! (Well, you'd want protection too, wouldn't you?)

Let's ask
Vamos a preguntar
💬 bamos a pray-goontar

bus
el autobús
💬 el owtoboos

78

Is it far?

¿Está lejos?

💋 esta lay-hos

Are we allowed in here?

¿Nos dejan entrar aquí?

💋 nos day-han entrar akee

car

el coche

💋 el kochay

You could gain a lot of street cred with your new Spanish friends by using a bit of slang.
A clapped-out car is ***"una cafetera"*** (*oona cafaytayra*), which means "coffee pot"! Try this: ***"¡Vaya cafetera!"*** (*baya cafaytayra* – "What an old banger!").

79

Park yourself here

swings los columpios
los koloom-peeyos

climbing frame el juego para escalar el hway-go para eska-lar

playground el patio de recreo
el pateeyo day rekrayo

grass la hierba
la yairba

tree el árbol
el ar-bol

slide
el tobogán
el tobogan

park el parque el parkay

Can we play ball games?

¿Podemos jugar a la pelota?

🗣 poday-mos hoo-gar a la pay-lota

roundabout

el tiovivo

🗣 el tio-beebo

sandpit

el arenero

🗣 el arain-airo

Can I have a go? ¿Puedo intentarlo?

🗣 pwaydo intain-tarloe

Picnics

I hate wasps

Odio las avispas

🗣 odeeyo las abeespas

Move over!

¡Apártate!

🗣 apar-tatay

bread

el pan 🗣 el pan

Shall we sit here?

¿Nos sentamos aquí?

🗣 nos sentamos akee

napkin

la servilleta

🗣 la serbeeyeta

ham el jamón

🗣 el hamon

cheese

el queso

🗣 el kayso

yoghurt

el yogurt

🗣 el yogurt

crisps

las patatas fritas

🗣 las patatas freetas

82

drinks

las bebidas

🐛 las bebeedas

knife

el cuchillo

🐛 el koocheeyo

spoon

la cuchara

🐛 la koochara

fork

el tenedor

🐛 el tenaydor

wasps

las avispas

🐛 las abeespas

bees

las abejas

🐛 las abayhas

bzzzz

ants

las hormigas

🐛 las ormeegas

Wake up, campers!

tent la tienda
🗣 la tyen-da

tent peg
la piqueta
🗣 la pee-kayta

camper van
la caravana
🗣 la kara-vana

penknife
la navaja de bolsillo
🗣 la nava-ha day bol-seelyo

camping stove
el camping gas
🗣 el "camping gas"

sleeping bag el saco de dormir
🗣 el sak-ko day door-meer

torch la linterna
🗣 la lintair-na

That tent's a palace!
Jo, ¡vaya tienda!
👄 ho, buy-ya tyen-da

Is there a campfire?
¿Hay una hoguera?
👄 ay oona og-waira

I've lost my torch
He perdido mi linterna
👄 eh pairdeedo mee lintair-na

These showers are gross!
¡Las duchas están sucias!
👄 las doo-chas estan soothyas

Where does the rubbish go?
¿Dónde se tira la basura?
👄 donday say teera la basoora

85

All the fun of the fair

big wheel
la noria
🗨 la noreeya

helter-skelter
el tobogán
🗨 el tobogan

house of mirrors
la casa de los espejos
🗨 la kasa day los espayhos

bumper cars
los coches de choque
🗨 los kochays
day chokay

Shall we go on this?
¿Nos montamos en éste?
🗨 nos montamos en estay

el pulpo

🗨 el poolpo

It's very fast

Va muy rápido

🗨 ba mwee rapeedo

That's for babies

Eso es para los pequeños

🗨 eso es para los pekay-nyos

Do you get wet in here?

¿En éste te mojas?

🗨 en estay tay mohas

I'm not going on my own

Yo solo no me monto

🗨 yo solo no may monto

Disco nights

mirror ball
la bola de espejos
🗣 la bola day espay–hos

loudspeaker
el altavoz
🗣 el altab–oth

Can I request a song?
¿Puedo pedir una canción?
🗣 pwaydo paydeer oona kan–thyon

The music is really lame
¡La música es malísima!
🗣 la mooseeka es malee–seema

DJ
el pinchadiscos
🗣 el peencha–deeskos

spotlights
los focos
🗣 los fo–kos

turntable
el tocadiscos
🗣 el toka–deeskos

How old do I need to be?

¿Cuántos años hay que tener?

🗨 kwantos anyos ay kay tenair

dance floor

la pista de baile

🗨 la peesta day balay

Let's dance!

¡Vamos a bailar!

🗨 ba-mos a balar

I love this song!

¡Me encanta esta canción!

🗨 may enkanta esta kan-thyon

89

POCKET MONEY

sweets
los caramelos
👄 los karamaylos

T-shirts
las camisetas
👄 las kameesetas

toys
los juguetes
👄 los hoogetes

el tendero
👄 el tendayro

books

los libros

 los leebros

el móvil

🫦 el mobeel

pencils

los lápices

🫦 los lapeethes

POCKET MONEY

What does that sign say?

butcher shop
carnicería
👄 karneethereeya

cake shop
pastelería
👄 pasteler
-reeya

bakery
panadería
👄 panadereeya

sweet shop
confitería
👄 confeeter-reeya

stationers
papelería
👄 papelereeya

greengrocer
verdulería
👄 berdooler-reeya

clothes shop
boutique
👄 booteek

Do you have some cash?

¿Tienes pasta?

💬 tee-enes pasta

I'm broke

No tengo un duro

💬 no tengo oon dooro

I'm loaded

Estoy forrado

💬 estoy forrado

Here you go

Aquí tienes

💬 akee tee-enes

That's a weird shop!

¡Vaya tienda más rara!

💬 buy-ya tyen-da mas ra-ra

That's a bargain Eso es una ganga

💬 eso es oona ganga

It's a rip-off

Es un robo

💬 es oon robo

93

Sweet heaven!

I love this shop

Me encanta esta tienda

👄 may enkanta esta tee-enda

Let's get some sweets

Vamos a comprar chucherías

👄 bamos a comprar choochereeyas

Let's get some ice cream

Vamos por un helado

👄 bamos por oon aylado

lollipops

las piruletas

👄 las peerooletas

a bar of chocolate

una tableta de chocolate

👄 oona tableta day chokolatay

chewing gum

el chicle

👄 el cheeklay

94

If you really want to look Spanish and end up with lots of fillings, ask for:

regaliz
🗣 (regaleez)

soft licorice sticks, available in red or black

polvos pica-pica

🗣 (polvos peeka peeka)

tangy fizzy sherbet sold in small packets with a lollipop to dip in

jamones
🗣 (hamon-nes)

fruity, fizzy gums in the shape of hams ("ham" is *jamón*)

Chupa-chups®

🗣 (choopa-choops)

lollies famous all over the world, but they come from Spain

nubes 🗣 (noobes)

soft marshmallow sweets ("flumps") in different shades (*nubes* means clouds)

kilométrico
🗣 (keelomay-treeko)

chewing gum in a strip like dental floss – pretend to the adults that you're flossing your teeth!

Other things you could buy
(that won't ruin your teeth!)

What are you getting?

¿Qué te vas a comprar?

👄 kay tay bas a komprar

That toy, please

Ese juguete, por favor

👄 esay hoogetay, por fabor

Two postcards, please

Dos postales, por favor

👄 dos postal-
les, por fabor

This is rubbish

Esto es una porquería

👄 esto es oona
porkayreeya

This is cool

Esto mola

👄 esto mola

I'm getting ...

Voy a comprar

👄 boy a comprar

... a pen

... un boli

👄 oon bolee

... stamps

... sellos

👄 seyos

... felt-tip pens

... rotuladores

👄 rotoolador-res

Lápices de Colores

... coloured pencils

... lápices de colores

👄 lapeethes day kolor-res

... a key ring

... un llavero

👄 oon yabairo

... comics

... tebeos

👄 taybayos

97

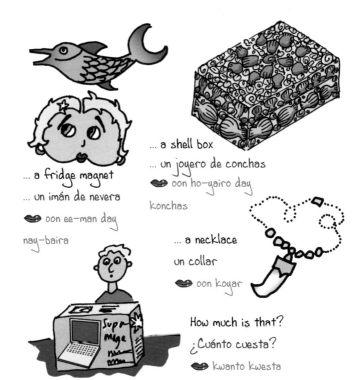

... a fridge magnet

... un imán de nevera

🗣 oon ee-man day nay-baira

... a shell box

... un joyero de conchas

🗣 oon ho-yairo day konchas

... a necklace

un collar

🗣 oon koyar

How much is that?

¿Cuánto cuesta?

🗣 kwanto kwesta

For many years Spain's favourite comics have been *Mortadelo y Filemón*, two accident-prone TIA agents (<u>not</u> CIA) and *Zipi y Zape*, two very naughty twins. Children also like to read *Mafalda*, an Argentinian comic, *Carlitos y Snoopy* (Charlie Brown & Snoopy), Tintin, Astérix and *¿Dónde está Wally?* (Where's Wally?).

Money talks

How much pocket money do you get?

¿Cuánto te dan de paga?

🐚 kwanto tay dan day pa-ga

I only have this much

Sólo tengo esto

🐚 soul-lo tain-go esto

Can you lend me ten euros?

¿Me prestas diez euros?

🐚 may praystas deeyeth ay-ooros

No way!

¡Ni hablar!

🐚 nee ablar

Spanish money is the **euro** (pronounced *ay-ooro*).
A euro is divided into 100 **centimos** (*thainteemos*).
Coins: 1, 2, 5, 10, 20, 50 **centimos**
        1, 2 **euros**
Notes: 5, 10, 20, 50, 100 **euros**
Make sure you know how much you are spending
before you blow all your pocket money at once!

Help!

Something has dropped/broken

Algo se ha caído/roto

🗨 algo say a kigh—eedo/roto

Please

Por favor

🗨 por fabor

Can you help me?

¿Me puedes ayudar?

🗨 may pwedes ayoodar

Where's the post box?

¿Dónde está el buzón?

🗨 donday esta el boothon

Where are the toilets?

¿Dónde están los aseos?

🗨 donday estan los asayos

I can't manage it

No puedo

🗣 no pwedo

Could you pass me that?

¿Me pasas eso?

🗣 may pasas eso

What time is it?

¿Qué hora es?

🗣 kay ora es

Come and see

Ven a ver

🗣 ben a bair

May I look at your watch?

¿Me deja que mire su reloj?

🗣 may deha kay meera soo reloh

103

Lost for words

I've lost ...

He perdido ...

👄 eh perdeedo

... my ticket

mi billete

👄 mee beeyaytay

... my parents

mis padres

👄 mees padrays

... my mobile

mi móvil

👄 mee mo-beel

... my shoes
mis zapatos

🗣 mees thapatos

... my money mi dinero

🗣 mee deenayro

... my jumper
mi jersey

🗣 mee hersay

... my watch
mi reloj

🗣 mee reloh

... my jacket mi chaqueta

🗣 mee chakayta

Adults only!

Show this page to adults who can't seem to make themselves clear (it happens). They will point to a phrase, you read what they mean, and you should all understand each other perfectly.

No te preocupes
Don't worry

Siéntate aquí
Sit down here

¿Tu nombre y apellidos?
What's your name and surname?

¿Cuántos años tienes?
How old are you?

¿De dónde eres?
Where are you from?

¿Dónde te alojas?
Where are you staying?

¿Dónde te duele?
Where does it hurt?

¿Eres alérgico a algo?
Are you allergic to anything?

Está prohibido
It's forbidden

Tiene que acompañarte un adulto
You have to have an adult with you

Voy por alguien que hable inglés
I'll get someone who speaks English

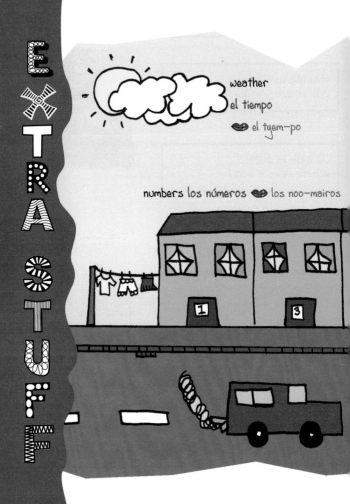

EXTRA STUFF

weather
el tiempo
el tyem-po

numbers los números los noo-mairos

1   3

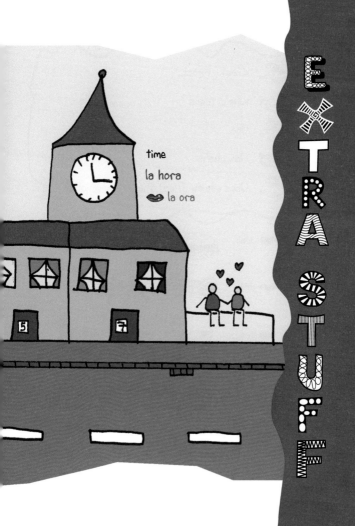

time

la hora

🫦 la ora

Numbers

Knock, knock.

Who's there?

Uno.

Uno who?

Unos where I got this crummy joke!

1 uno oono

2 dos dos

3 tres trays

4 cuatro kwatro

5 cinco theenko

6 seis sayis

7 siete see-etay

8 ocho ocho

9 nueve nwebay

10 diez deeyeth

11 once onthay

12 doce dothay

trece 👄 trethay

catorce 👄 katorthay

quince 👄 keenthay

16	dieciséis	*deeyethee sayis*
17	diecisiete	*deeyethee see-etay*
18	dieciocho	*deeyethee ocho*
19	diecinueve	*deeyethee nwebay*

If you want to say "thirty-two", "fifty-four" and so on, you can just put the two numbers together like you do in English. But don't forget to add the word for "and" (**y** – *ee*) in the middle:

32	treinta y dos	*traynta ee dos*
54	cincuenta y cuatro	*theenkwenta ee kwatro*
81	ochenta y uno	*ochenta ee oono*

20	viente	*baintay*
30	treinta	*traynta*
40	cuarenta	*kwarenta*
50	cincuenta	*theenkwenta*
60	sesenta	*saysenta*
70	setenta	*saytenta*
80	ochenta	*ochenta*
90	noventa	*nobenta*
100	cien	*theeyen*

a thousand mil *meel*

a million un millón *oon meel-yon*

a gazillion! tropecientos! *tropay- theeyentos*

1st	primero	*preemairo*
2nd	segundo	*segoondo*
3rd	tercero	*terthayro*
4th	cuarto	*kwarto*
5th	quinto	*keento*
6th	sexto	*sexto*
7th	séptimo	*septeemo*
8th	octavo	*octabo*
9th	noveno	*nobayno*
10th	décimo	*daytheemo*

Fancy a date?

If you want to say a date in Spanish, you don't need to use 1st, 2nd, etc. Just say the ordinary number followed by *de* (*day*):

Lunes	Martes	Miércoles	Jueves	Viernes	Sábado	Domingo
		1	2	3	4	5
6	7	8	9	10	11	12
13	14	15	16	17	18	19
20	21	22	23	24	25	26
27	28	29	30			

uno de marzo   (1st of March)

diez de julio   (10th of July)

Months

March	marzo	*martho*
April	abril	*abreel*
May	mayo	*my-yo*

June	junio	*hooneeyo*
July	julio	*hooleeyo*
August	agosto	*agosto*

September	septiembre	*septee-embray*
October	octubre	*octoobray*
November	noviembre	*nobee-embray*

December	diciembre	*deethee-embray*
January	enero	*enayro*
February	febrero	*febrayro*

Seasons

primavera   *preemabayra*

verano   *berano*

otoño   *otonyo*

invierno   *eenbee-erno*

118

Days of the week

Monday	lunes	*loon-nes*
Tuesday	martes	*mar-tes*
Wednesday	miércoles	*mee-erkol-les*
Thursday	jueves	*hoo-ebes*
Friday	viernes	*bee-er-nes*
Saturday	sábado	*sabado*
Sunday	domingo	*domeengo*

By the way, Spanish kids have a two-and-a-half hour lunch break! Time enough for lunch and a siesta. But they don't finish until 5pm in the afternoon.

Good times

It's ...
Son ...
💋 sonn

(five) o'clock
las (cinco)
💋 las (theenko)

quarter past (two)
las (dos) y cuarto
💋 las (dos) ee kwarto

quarter to (four)
las (cuatro) menos cuarto
💋 las (kwatro) menos kwarto

half past (three)
las (tres) y media
💋 las (trays) ee medya

five past (ten)

las (diez) y cinco

👄 las (deeyeth) ee theenko

twenty past (eleven)

las (once) y viente

👄 las (onthay) ee baintay

ten to (four)

las (cuatro) menos diez

👄 las (kwatro) menos deeyeth

twenty to (six)

las (seis) menos veinte

👄 las (sayis) menos baintay

Watch out for "one o'clock". It's a bit different from the other times. If you want to say "It's one o'clock" you have to say **_Es la una_** (*es la oona*). "It's half past one" is **_Es la una y media_** (*es la oona ee medya*), and so on.

morning
mañana
🗣 la manyarna

midday
mediodía
🗣 el medyo-deeya

afternoon
la tarde
🗣 la tarday

midnight
la medianoche
🗣 la medya-nochay

evening la noche
🗣 la nochay

now ahora
🗣 a-ora

night
la noche
🗣 la nochay

today
hoy
🗣 oy

yesterday
ayer
🗣 ayair

tomorrow
mañana
🗣 manyarna

123

Weather wise

Can we go out?

¿Podemos salir fuera?

💋 podaymos saleer fwera

It's hot

Hace calor

💋 athay kalor

It's cold

Hace frío

💋 athay freeyo

It's horrible

Hace un día horrible

💋 athay oon deeya orreeblay

It's raining seas!

In Spanish it doesn't rain "cats and dogs", it rains "seas"! That's what they say when it's raining really heavily:

¡Está lloviendo a mares! *esta yobeeyendo a mar-res*

It's windy

Hace viento

 athay beeyento

It's sunny

Hace sol

athay sol

It's raining

Está lloviendo

esta yobeeyendo

It's snowing

Está nevando

esta nebando

It's nice Hace bueno

athay bweno

I'm soaked

Estoy empapado

estoy empapardo

125

Signs of life

altura mínima

minimum Height

Móviles
prohibidos
No mobiles

Entrada prohibida
No entry

Sólo mayores
de 18

Over 18s only

Sólo menores de 5
Under 5s only

NO FUNCIONA

OUT OF ORDER

PRIVATE
Privado

Caballeros

Señoras

128